Quick Tips! Morning Message

BY ANNE ADAMS, DIANE FARNHAM, CAROL McQUILLEN, AND DONNA PEABODY

SCHOLASTIC
PROFESSIONAL BOOKS

NEW YORK • TORONTO • LONDON • AUCKLAND • SYDNEY
MEXICO CITY • NEW DELHI • HONG KONG • BUENOS AIRES

*Dedicated to all the Superstars who have shone their light at
Orchard School over the years.*

*With special thanks to our editor, Joan Novelli,
and our families for their support.*

Edited by **Joan Novelli**
Cover design by **Maria Lilja**
Cover illustration by **Dave Clegg**
Interior design by **Holly Grundon**
Interior illustrations by **James Graham Hale**
with additional illustrations by Paige Billin-Frye, Maxie Chambliss, Shelley Dieterichs, Rusty Fletcher, Tammie Lyon, and Ellen Joy Sasaki
ISBN: 0-439-37667-x

2 3 4 5 6 7 8 9 10   40   10 09 08 07 06 05 04 03

Contents

Teaching With Morning Messages 4

    Format Variations 5

    Management Tips 6

    Assessment Strategies 8

**Building Community
With Morning Messages** 10

**Supporting Literacy
With Morning Messages** 13

    Reproducible Activity Pages 28–33

**Meeting the Math Standards
With Morning Messages** 34

    Reproducible Activity Pages 44–48

**Strengthening Science Concepts
With Morning Messages** 49

    Reproducible Activity Pages 60–63

**Celebrating Special Days
With Morning Messages** 64

    Reproducible Activity Pages 76–80

Teaching
With Morning Messages

It's 8:20 A.M. and Kevin greets his teacher as he enters the classroom. He follows his morning routine of taking care of his belongings and checking in for lunch, then heads over to the morning message and begins to read. Today's message welcomes children, lets them know a little about their day, and invites them to respond to a question about a cricket they've been observing: *Do you think the cricket is a male or female?* Kevin places an X in the male category, helping to create a class graph of responses. Later that day, the class will revisit the graph and discuss the data, strengthening math and science skills while building literacy.

Children eagerly anticipate each day's morning message. At the end of the day, they make sure to turn the easel paper to a fresh page to get ready for tomorrow's message. Morning messages enhance teaching and learning in many ways, among them providing for:

- powerful communication between teacher and students, and student to student.

- literacy skills practice across the curriculum.

- daily opportunities to respond to print.

- interaction with text and other students, and with the whole class.

- quick assessment of skills and of the ways children approach tasks.

- opportunities to collect data on children's thinking and feelings.

This book offers how-tos for making morning messages a meaningful part of your classroom routine. From management tips to dozens of ready-to-use messages that connect with literacy, math, science, special days, and more, this book will help make morning messages a favorite part of your students' day.

More capable readers can assist their classmates in reading the morning message. Parents who bring their children to school can also help.

○ ○ ○

Format Variations

The fun of creating meaningful messages is partly due to the variety of formats in which children can respond. Just as in any personal communication, there is no set way to present a message. Students are excited to read and respond to a fresh piece of writing each morning. You can be certain they will look for the morning message as part of their expected routines. Children will let you know if the morning message is missing!

You can vary the complexity of the morning message format according to your students' varying levels of literacy and your intent. Young learners benefit from predictable morning message formats. Predictable patterns in the text and rebus pictures are two ways to make the task approachable. Older children enjoy the challenges of more detailed and complex messages. In fact, they can create the morning messages over time within whatever guidelines the teacher sets in motion. Browse the ideas that follow to inspire new formats unique to your style of teaching!

Friendly Letters

Friendly letters with no response required can be effective when students have an early commitment in the day (such as physical education) and will not have time to compose a written response. The personal message can be an opportunity to share a compliment, tell about the day, or give an important directive to set the day on a smooth path.

Graphic Organizers

Graphs can be used to record each child's response to a question or specific inquiry. They are useful to get a quick snapshot of each student's thinking and can be used during a lesson or meeting time later in the day. It's fun to teach tally marks, Xs, and other symbols to represent individual responses.

Mini Works of Art

Drawings, paintings, and other artistic representations provide a personal, creative response that can serve as a discussion prompt later in the day. Artistic responses can also become writing prompts for a follow-up lesson.

The reproducible activity pages in each section are designed to stretch students' learning and build independence. For example, a morning message that invites children to count chairs in the classroom (page 36) is supported by an activity (page 44) children can complete on their own, counting other objects in the classroom. Pattern pages are another way to enrich children's morning message experiences. From birthday balloons to rockets, patterns are an effective and fun way to have children respond to questions.

○ ○ ○

Sticky Note Responses

Sticky notes are especially useful when you want to be certain that children are each doing their own thinking about the prompt. After reading the message, have children take a large sticky note back to their tables or desks and write their name on the front and their response on the back. This also solves a time- and space-management problem—children can work at a table rather than crowd around the easel waiting for a turn. (Note: The top of the sticky note back has adhesive on it, but on large notes there is plenty of room beneath this for children to record responses.)

Clothespin Clip-Ons

Clothespins are a helpful way to get a quick recording of student preferences. Some teachers like to have clothespins handy with each child's name on them. (Write each child's name on a plastic or wood spring-type clothespin with a permanent or paint marker.) This is an especially helpful format for young learners or when you are short on time.

Math Manipulative Messages

Math manipulatives can be useful for recording responses to a morning message question in a tactile format. Unifix cubes are just one possibility; children can use them to graph data. Children can also use manipulatives to show measurement, create patterns, represent solutions to math problems, and collect data.

Management Tips

"I can't see!" "There's no room for me!" "Can somebody please move?" Even a well-planned morning message will lose its effectiveness if students can't easily read it. Each classroom setting calls for unique management guidelines to ensure success for everyone. Implementing a morning message is no different. Following are questions and tips to consider as you set up your morning message routine.

Tip

Have students brainstorm greetings— for example, Dear, Hello, Good Morning, Hi, Welcome, Bonjour, and Happy Day! Rotate the greeting to include all appropriate suggestions.

○ ○ ○

Organizing Time

Ask yourself the following questions to help make sure that there's enough time for students to read and respond to a message and for you to use it as intended, whether as a simple greeting or as a springboard to a later lesson.

- What do you want to accomplish by using a morning message? (for example, friendly greeting, skill practice, lesson introduction, springboard for discussion, skill assessment)

- How long will students have in the morning to interact with the morning message?

- When will you review the morning message with the class as a whole? The same time each day? Flexible times? As an introduction to math, literacy, or another curriculum area?

Organizing Students

Make decisions about how many students can interact with the message at one time. Consider placing a masking tape line on the floor to indicate the message reading area. A taped line can also indicate where students will wait their turn. Identify a reader-leader for the day or week, whose job is to help others read and respond to the message. Practice reading the message with the reader-leader before others interact with it. To keep students moving along, be sure they know how many responses you would like—for example, you might need to explain that "Your favorite weekend activity" would mean only one. To give students plenty of time to respond, they can use sticky notes to write responses at their desks, then place them on the morning message.

Choosing Content

In addition to routine information, the content of your morning message might support a particular lesson, such as a science investigation or a math activity on shapes. Another approach is to create a "menu" for your messages—for example:

- Marvelous Math Monday: math task

- Terrific Tuesday: theme task

Tip

For morning messages that invite children to team up for conversations or other activities, try these ideas for partnering students:

- Have children find someone who is wearing the same color as they are that day.

- Cut small cards into two-piece puzzles. Write each child's name on one piece of a puzzle. Have children find their partners by putting the puzzles together.

- Write sets of words that rhyme on small cards, one word per card. Have children find their rhyming matches to meet their partners.

○ ○ ○

- Word Power Wednesday: literacy task

- Thoughtful Thursday: survey question

- Fun Friday: joke or riddle with the answer in code

When all else fails, have a message that simply reads: Draw a picture of something you would like to learn more about.

Supporting Students

Strategies for assisting students in reading the morning message include:

- Underline tricky words.

- Use pictures in the message for beginning readers.

- Write each sentence in a different color.

- Follow a consistent format, limiting the message to any combination of the following: date, greeting, leader of the day, task, news of the day, closing.

Assessment Strategies

Educators are constantly monitoring and adjusting their lessons to accommodate the developmental needs of their students. Morning messages provide teachers with a quick snapshot of children's thinking, whether they record responses in pictures, symbols, or words. Simply noting each student's approach to the morning message provides a wealth of information. Are children eager and confident in their approach? What organizational strategies do they employ? Since each message requires an individual response, teachers can also gather knowledge about each child's social and emotional levels: What are some ways in which children interact with one another at the easel?

An example of a message you might use at the beginning of the school year follows on page 9. To assess responses to the message, notice how children approach the task:

- What strategies do they use to read the message?

- Do they move from left to right as they read? Do they know how to return and sweep at the end of a line?

- Do they read the message silently or aloud? (If children read the message aloud, do they read fluently and with expression?)

- Are they aware of punctuation?

- What do they do when they come to an unknown word?

- Do they recognize sight words?

- Do they use a pointer to keep their place?

- Are they able to read and follow directions?

- What hand do children use to print? Are they having difficulty with dominance? Is their pencil grip firm? Do children print with ease, or is the task awkward for them?

- Do they use all uppercase letters or a mixture of upper- and lowercase?

- Are children experiencing reversals or problems with directionality while printing?

> Good Morning, Girls and Boys!
>
> Today is Friday, September 4. Please print your name. Count the number of letters in your name. Write that number next to your name.
>
> Mrs. Jarrett

Markers tend to bleed color onto the next sheet of paper on pads of easel paper. To avoid this, place a sheet of thin cardboard between pages to absorb the excess ink.

○ ○ ○

Morning messages are valuable skill-builders that help inform teachers about their students' needs and growth. While some teachers give the charts to children to take home, it's also fun to revisit these messages with children throughout the year to highlight their progress.

Building Community
With Morning Messages

> Good Morning,
>
> Today is Tuesday, September 18.
> Taking care of one another is
> one of our classroom practices.
> Draw a picture that shows
> how you care for someone.
>   Sincerely,
>   Mr. Clarke

Kathryn skips into the classroom holding on tightly to a baggie of photographs. "Is Paul here yet? I have a special present for him." Kathryn explains that she and her family spent the weekend at a natural history museum and they were able to take some pictures of the dinosaur skeletons. She knows how much Paul loves dinosaurs and mentions that last week on the morning message he drew a dinosaur as his favorite animal. Now she has a picture to give him!

Morning messages are interactive springboards for community building. These messages are written to provide opportunities for teamwork, social-skills practice, and cooperation. They serve as an

engaging tool to pave the way for developing a positive climate in the classroom. Morning messages that are well composed at the start of each day foster a connection between children in their classroom community.

Sample Morning Message Prompts

◎ We have an American flag hanging in our classroom. Please add a star or a stripe to this picture of the American flag.

NOTE TO TEACHER: You may draw a partially complete flag, leaving enough missing stars and stripes so that each child can complete one. Or you may choose to complete the flag at morning meeting, incorporating math skills to find out, for example, how many more stars children need to add.

◎ We are going on a field trip today. Do you think the bus driver would like to hear loud voices or soft voices? Put an X in the appropriate column.

◎ If you could do something nice for your friend, what would it be? Draw a picture and label your idea.

◎ [Name] is our school nurse [principal, cafeteria helper, custodian]. She works hard to help us stay healthy. Today we will give her this thank-you card. Please sign your name.

◎ We have class meeting every morning. What part do you like best? Write your name in the column that matches your choice: Song, Greeting, News, Problem-Solving.

◎ We have a new student joining us next week. Draw a picture showing how you will make him feel welcome.

◎ When we greet each other, we make friendly eye contact. Greet two classmates this morning. Write their names next to yours.

◎ Imagine that there is not enough room in our morning circle. Draw a picture of yourself solving this problem.

Morning messages are a good way to let children share things they want to discuss with you or their class-mates. You can inquire by writing: Do you have anything you want to share at our class meeting time? Children can write down their ideas (without neces-sarily signing their names). Their topics then become part of the meeting agenda.

○ ○ ○

Book Link

In *Little Beaver and the Echo,* by Amy MacDonald (Putnam, 1990), a young beaver sets out across the pond to make friends with a distant, lonely voice and meets many new friends along the way. This is a great story for the beginning of a school year, when many children are concerned about making new friends. Pair this story with *So What?* by Miriam Cohen (Bantam Doubleday Dell, 1982), a light-hearted look at having the courage to be yourself. Follow up with a morning message that invites children to tell one way that they are a good friend.

◎ You would like to join a group of classmates building with blocks. In a bubble, write some words you could use to join in.

NOTE TO TEACHER: Draw a word bubble for each child beneath the message.

◎ We place our right hand on our heart when we say the pledge each morning. Trace your right hand and write your name in it.

◎ Draw a star under your favorite choice for indoor recess.

NOTE TO TEACHER: Set up a simple chart with headings for several activities, such as Songs, Games, and Reading.

◎ We are alike in some ways. We are different, too. What is your favorite _____ [food, pet, animal, color, number, lunch, candy, holiday, song, part of the school day, book, game, toy]? Write your answer next to your name. Find someone who has a different answer. Share reasons for choosing these as your favorites.

Supporting Literacy
With Morning Messages

Hi, Superstars!

Today is Monday, April 17. Jodi is our leader. Today we will read <u>The Very Hungry Caterpillar</u>, by Eric Carle. Do you think a hungry caterpillar would like something from your lunch today? Write an X under Yes or No. Write your name next to the X.

       Sincerely,

       Ms. Thomas

As Molly enters the classroom, she puts her backpack in her cubby and checks in for lunch. She knows the next step is to read the morning message. She looks for her partner, who assists her as she points to each word and reads. Molly finds out who the day's leaders are, and then responds to a question about a story the class will share at literacy time.

While many teachers use the morning message to focus on the mechanics of writing, the possibilities for building literacy skills are endless. This section focuses on specific skills in language arts and how you can use the morning message to support your students' growth in those areas.

Phonological Awareness

Phonological awareness is one of the building blocks for reading success. Phonological awareness includes the understanding that words are made up of separate sounds (phonemic awareness). It also encompasses recognition of larger units within words, such as rhyming chunks, and words in sentences. Rhymes, songs, and word games are familiar and fun ways to build phonological awareness. Morning messages are another way to weave phonological awareness activities into the school day, while at the same time exposing children to print.

Using the sample below as a model, substitute any of the following variations in your morning message to support your teaching goals.

Dear Children,

Today will be a sunny spring day. We will plant seeds with our Book Buddies. Draw a picture of something that rhymes with <u>spring</u>.

Sincerely,

Mr. Hale

Sample Morning Message Prompts

◎ Draw a picture of something that rhymes with *at* [*ink*, *big*, and so on].

◎ Look at the picture. Say the word. Draw a picture of something that starts with the same sound.

> *NOTE TO TEACHER: Draw a picture to represent a word that starts with a consonant sound you are teaching—for example, draw a butterfly to represent the /b/ sound.*

◎ How many beats (syllables) are in the word *watermelon*? Write the number on the back of a sticky note. Sign your name on the front.

> *NOTE TO TEACHER: You may wish to draw a picture to assist students in reading the word.*

Count the Beats, pages 28–29

◎ Draw a picture of a word that has two beats (syllables).

> *NOTE TO TEACHER: For an independent follow-up, see On My Own: Count the Beats, pages 28–29. Help children follow these steps: Cut around three sides of each picture to make a flap. Place glue around the edges of the back of this page. Place the picture page on the word page and press together. Look at each picture. Say the word and count the beats. Lift up the flap and write the number of beats.*

◎ Draw pictures of two words that rhyme.

◎ How many beats are in your name? Print your name under the correct number below.

> *NOTE TO TEACHER: Set up columns beneath the morning message with number headings to represent syllables in children's names.*

Book Link

Share "The House That Jack Built." Then treat students to ***The Book That Jack Wrote***, by Jon Scieszka (Viking, 1994), a whimsical takeoff on the original nursery rhyme. Pair the book with a morning message that lets children complete sets of rhyming words from the book or from nursery rhymes referenced in it.

Letters From A to Z

> Hello!
>
> Today we have a school assembly. Tomorrow we will go to the pumpkin patch. Draw a picture of something that begins with the letter *p*.
>
> Sincerely,
> Mrs. Harris

Tip

Varying the morning message gives children experience with different types of reading. Likewise, providing for a changing display of books in the classroom encourages variety in the stories children select. Cycle in new books by familiar authors as well as new authors, illustrators, and genres.

Part of building a literate classroom environment is giving children opportunities to practice letters and their sounds throughout the day. A morning message lets you start the day with this kind of experience. It also provides an opportunity to informally assess both children's strategies for finding letters they need when they are stuck and their fluency in writing. Here are some ready-to-use morning messages for teaching letter recognition and sounds.

Sample Morning Message Prompts

◉ Find your name. Draw a circle around the first letter [the last letter, the third letter].

NOTE TO TEACHER: *Print each child's name below the message.*

◎ Draw a picture of a word that begins with the letter ___.

◎ Fill in only one of the missing letters in today's message.

NOTE TO TEACHER: *Draw a fill-in line in place of enough letters in the morning message so that each child can fill in one.*

◎ Write your favorite letter of the alphabet. Cut out a picture from a magazine to show something that starts with that letter. Glue it next to your letter.

◎ Write the matching lowercase letter next to an uppercase letter.

NOTE TO TEACHER: *Write the uppercase letters below the message. Follow up with On My Own: Letter Match, page 30.*

◎ We are learning alphabetical order. Fill in one of the missing letters.

NOTE TO TEACHER: *Write the alphabet in order several times, leaving out enough letters so that each child can fill in one missing letter.*

◎ How many letters are in our alphabet? Write the number on the back of a sticky note. Write your name on the front of the sticky note.

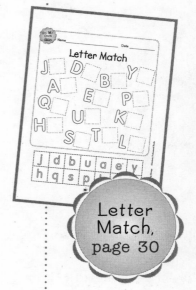

Letter Match, page 30

Words

Building knowledge of words for both recognition and meaning enhances the skills necessary to communicate—through reading, writing, speaking, and listening. Giving children opportunities to play with words is a fun way to encourage this growth. Try the ideas on page 18 to incorporate wordplay in your morning messages. Just add the wordplay activity to the information you usually include, or make it the focus.

Hi, Superstars!

Shavani's mother will be our guest reader today. We will be making thank-you cards for her. Practice writing your name in fancy letters.

Sincerely,

Miss Casey

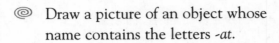

✦ Draw a picture of an object whose name contains the letters -at.

NOTE TO TEACHER: As the photo shows, the complete morning message highlights words that contain the -at chunk.

✦ Find a word that begins with the same letter as _____. Circle it!

NOTE TO TEACHER: Write words beneath the morning message, some of which begin with the target letter. Make sure there is one for each child.

✦ Find your name. Trace it and draw a circle around it.

NOTE TO TEACHER: This message works well for emergent readers and writers, helping them to recognize the letters in their name and practice writing it.

✦ Find a sticky note with your name on it. On the back of the sticky note, write a word for the opposite of *night.*

NOTE TO TEACHER: Place large sticky notes beneath the message area. Write each child's name on a note. Have children take their note to their desks, write their word on it, then stick the note back on the morning message.

✦ Write a word that means the same thing as _____.

NOTE TO TEACHER: Complete the sentence with a target word. You might also suggest that students consult a thesaurus.

✦ Write a word that has something in common with the word _____.

NOTE TO TEACHER: Fill in a word for children to respond to. They might write a word that has a similar spelling pattern, consonant cluster, meaning, and so on.

✦ Write the longest word you know.

Tip

As young learners discover the magic of words, there's nothing like having good picture dictionaries available for further exploration. Children can use picture dictionaries as sources of words or for reference in illustrating pictures for their stories.

○ ○ ○

- Cut out a friendship word from a magazine and paste it on the message. Outline the shape of your word with a marker.

- Invent a word of your choice and be ready to share what it means at morning meeting.

- Write a synonym for the word *fantastic* in a box below.

  NOTE TO TEACHER: *Draw a box beneath the message for each child.*

- Put the following words in alphabetical order under one of the sticky notes below: *north, south, east, west.* Write your name on the front of the sticky note.

  NOTE TO TEACHER: *Place a sticky note beneath the message for each child.*

- Trace and cut out a star. Write a word about our study of [fill in a theme students are studying]. Tell what it means. You can use a dictionary. Glue your star to the border of our morning message.

  NOTE TO TEACHER: *Provide star templates for children to trace.*

Phonics

Learning to identify words quickly and accurately leads to fluency in reading, which fosters a love of literature—one of the goals of any reading program. Explicit phonics instruction helps children acquire the skills they need to decode words—including recognizing them by sight, sounding them out, and using context clues and structural analysis. It is also essential to weave phonics skills into daily activities for practice—for example, with morning messages. Try adding any of the following interactive tasks to your morning message to strengthen phonics skills.

Hi, Readers!

Emma will be our leader.
Ashley will be our line checker.
Read the words on the word wall with a friend.

Sincerely,
Mr. Shim

Sample Morning Message Prompts

◉ Count the consonants in our morning message today. Write that number next to your name.

◉ Find a short-*o* word in the morning message. Write another short-*o* word below.

◉ Put a box around one of the digraphs in today's message. [*sh, ch, th, wh, ph, gh, ng*]

◉ Write the words for one of the contractions below.

> ***Note to Teacher:*** *Below the message, write a contraction for each student. For a follow-up, see On My Own: Contraction Wheel, page 31. Help children cut out the wheels and the window on wheel A, place A on B, and attach with a brass fastener. Invite them to turn the wheel to match words with contractions.*

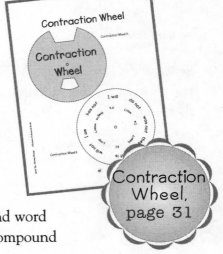

Contraction Wheel, page 31

◉ We have been learning about compound words. Find a compound word in today's message. Write a new compound word in a shape below.

> ***Note to Teacher:*** *Draw fun shapes beneath the message, one per child, for children to write their words in.*

◉ Count the vowels in this sentence: I am special! Write the number next to your name. Then circle the vowels in your name.

> ***Note to Teacher:*** *For a follow-up, see On My Own: I Am Special!, page 32.*

I Am Special!, page 32

Tip

Using the morning message to make discoveries about print is a powerful whole group activity. It encourages students to focus on print and gives them time together to share what they learn.

○ ○ ○

Concepts of Print

Good Morning, Readers and Writers,

I enjoyed reading your journals last night.
Please take out your journal. Read an entry to
a partner. Tell one thing you enjoyed about your
partner's journal entry.

     Sincerely,

     Mrs. Nyarko

Young readers continue to build knowledge of text through exposure and direct instruction, along with practice. Morning messages give children opportunities to read and interpret text. These messages also become tools for analyzing print with individual students, in small groups, and in whole-group instruction. Try these ideas to invite children to read and interpret text with the morning message. Add the interactive tasks to the regular part of your message, or make it the focus of the message, as with the sample message above.

Sample Morning Message Prompts

◎ How many sentences are in this message? Write your name under the correct number below.

◎ Which of the above sentences need quotations? Sign your name below the appropriate sentence numbers.

How many misspelled words can you find? Write your name under that number.

NOTE TO TEACHER: Include columns with number headings.

Write a greeting you would like me to use in one of our morning messages. Sign your name next to it.

Change one of the upper- or lowercase letters to make a needed correction. Use a small piece of correction tape.

Show how you are becoming a powerful writer. Choose a piece of notepaper. Take a name out of the hat. Write a friendly note to that person.

NOTE TO TEACHER: Write children's names on slips of paper and place them in a hat for children to select randomly. Provide assorted notepaper.

Writing

The morning message is a practical way to let students know what you would like them to focus on in their writing experiences. Use the morning message to give students specific writing instruction. While some of these ideas don't require a response on the message board, allowing for one invites students to engage in a variety of writing formats. Here are some ready-to-use ideas for focusing on writing skills with your morning message.

Children love to see their name in print. Consider meaningful ways to include the names of the children in your class from time to time—for example, in birthday announcements, compliments, and class newsletters.

Dear Children,

Good morning! Today is the first day of a new week. Think about your weekend. List five events from your weekend that you could turn into stories.

Sincerely,

Mrs. Salvatore

Sample Morning Message Prompts

◎ Take a moment and add a sentence to our thank-you letter for _____. Draw your face in the border. Write your name just below your drawing.

◎ Write a message to your partner about his or her last journal entry. Write your comment on the next sheet of paper. Use at least three sentences.

◎ In your math journal, write a problem about the number of students in our class. Use a real situation or make up your own. Be creative!

◎ Write a compliment to your Book Buddy. Include at least _____ sentences.

◎ How do you feel today? Copy and complete this sentence: I feel _____ because _____.

◎ Write a note to put under the pillow of someone in your family. What do you feel good about these days? What would you like this person to know? Please show me your work. Then put it in your backpack.

◎ Sign your name next to the type of story you would like to write. Take a story map to your table. Start planning!

NOTE TO TEACHER: *Label a chart beneath the message for responses: Adventure, Mystery, Fairy Tale, Other. Photocopy a class set of page 33 and place it with the morning message.*

Tip

To keep morning message motivation high, vary the writing tools available to students. Markers, colored pencils, gel pens, and crayons are all fun.

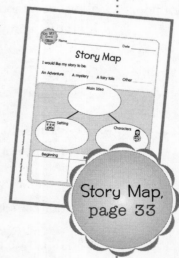

Story Map, page 33

Literature

> Good Morning!
>
> Today we will read a nonfiction book about trees. Write a sentence to tell something you know about trees. Write a question you have about trees.
>
> Sincerely,
>
> Mr. Ortiz

Tip

Sometimes it's helpful to check in on students' home reading with the morning message. You might ask students about their favorite place to read, favorite time to read, or perhaps the people they enjoy reading with at home.

○ ○ ○

The beauty of literature in a classroom is like the artistry of a well-designed backdrop in a stage production. It indeed sets the stage! Children who have inviting books at home and in their classrooms engage in reading more readily. It's fun to get a snapshot of each child's response to a particular book with a morning message. Using the sample above as a model, substitute any of the following sentences to make literature connections with your morning message.

Sample Morning Message Prompts

◎ What kind of book are you reading at home now? (fantasy, fiction, nonfiction, fairy tale, other) Draw a picture. Write the title.

◎ Draw what you think will happen in the next chapter of the book our class is reading.

◎ Illustrate a story scene from a favorite fairy tale. Write a sentence about it.

- It's been fun reading [book title] by [author's name]. Go to your Literature Response Log and write at least three sentences telling how [name two characters] get along.

- We have been reading many books by [author's name]. Go to the art center and create a new cover for your favorite [author's name] story.

- Your play yesterday of [book title] by [author's name] was just great! Go to your journal and draw a character from the play.

- I enjoyed sharing about friends yesterday after reading [book about friends], by [author's name]. Write a message to a friend.

Speaking and Listening

One of the ways to keep the morning message time short and sweet is to ask students to respond by speaking with a classmate. This approach doubles as a communication-skill builder—engaging children in purposeful conversations that can help build confidence and resolve conflicts. Add these ready-to-go conversation starters to your morning messages to build listening and speaking skills.

Hi, Classmates!

Today is cloudy so we will have to make our own sunshine. Get together with your partner and share something you like about him or her. Then get ready to plant bulbs outside!

Love,

Mrs. McQuillen

Tip

It's fun to invite guest readers to share a favorite book with students. These experiences provide rich opportunities for children to hear other voices and expression. We call our guest readers Royal Readers. They even wear a crown! Follow up with a morning message that lets children respond to the experience.

○ ○ ○

Sample Morning Message Prompts

◎ Invite a classmate to play a game with you at recess today.

◎ Give a compliment to one of your classmates. Choose a name below and mark it with an X. Sign your name next to the X.

◎ Look at your plant experiment. Be ready to give a report at our morning meeting.

◎ Pick a name from the jar. Tell that person what you read about at home last night.

◎ Find a classmate and agree on something to chat about at snack time.

◎ What would you like to know about your classmates? Write a question and put it in the box. We will use these questions tomorrow at class meeting.

NOTE TO TEACHER: Place a box at the morning message area for students' questions.

Drama

When young learners produce and perform their own stories, something powerful happens to the connections they make.

Hi, Players!

You did a great job with the play! Take a look at the pictures of the play on the table. Tell what you liked best.

Love,
Mrs. Franck

Whether the story is a playlet written by an individual, small group, or whole class, it is an invitation to engage all the senses. You can use morning messages to connect with children's dramatic experiences and gain insight into their thinking. Children's responses also serve as springboards for further discussion at your morning meeting. Try these suggestions for making drama connections with your morning message.

Sample Morning Message Prompts

◉ Have you ever been in a play before? Write your name under Yes or No.

◉ Complete this sentence: If I were in a play, I would like to be _____. (Write your answer and name below.)

◉ Draw a picture about a play you might like to write. Write your main idea.

◉ What one story or fairy tale do you think our class would have the most fun acting out? Write the title and tell why.

◉ Today we will act out *The Three Little Bears*, by Jan Brett. Please lend a hand and make sure the kitchen of our playhouse is set up for the story.

NOTE TO TEACHER: *Use any picture book that lends itself to a play format.*

Book Link

Share **Amazing Grace,** by Mary Hoffman (Dial, 1991), to meet a young girl who loves acting out stories. Young readers can easily identify with her as she is empowered to be her very best. Pair the story with this morning message: What [fairy tale, book] character would you like to be in a play? Write the character's name. Draw a picture of yourself as this character.

Name_____ Date _____

Count the Beats

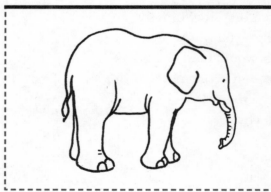

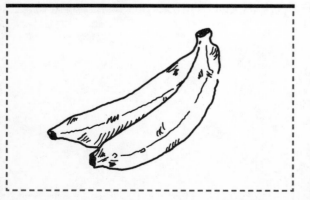

Quick Tips! Morning Message   Scholastic Professional Books

Name_____ Date _____

Count the Beats

watermelon	cake
_____	_____
train	elephant
_____	_____
bananas	flowers
_____	_____

Name_____ Date_____

Letter Match

Contraction Wheel

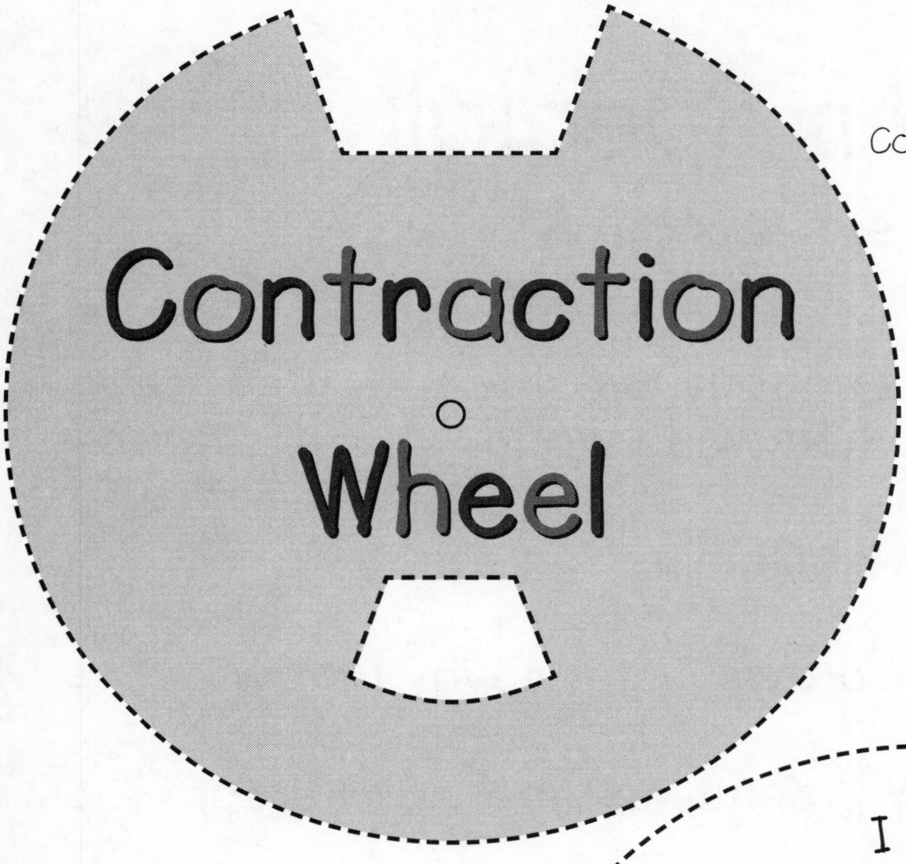

Contraction Wheel A

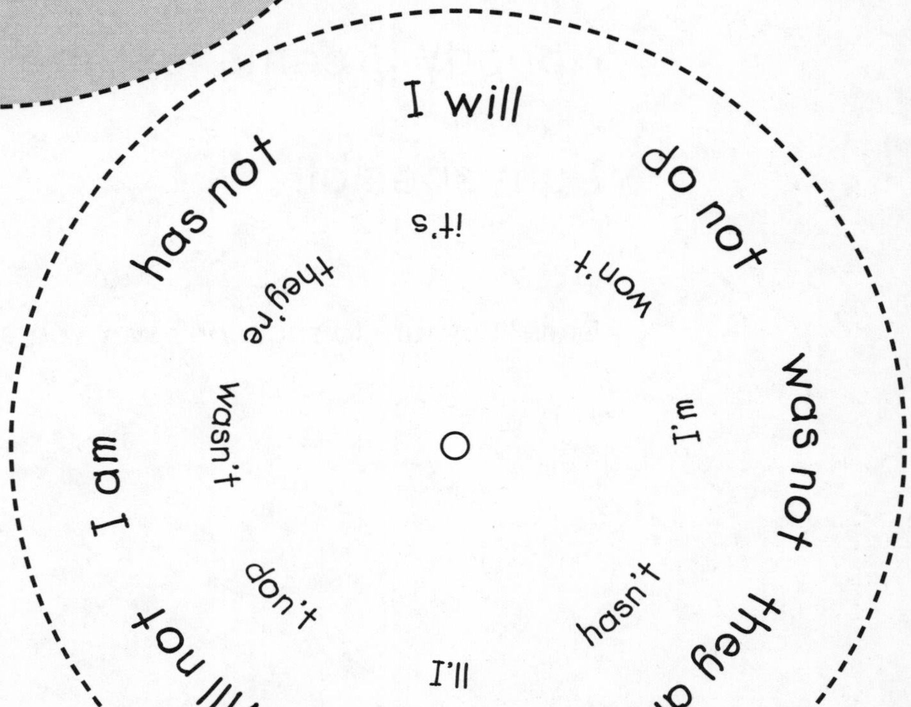

Contraction
°
Wheel

Contraction Wheel B

I will

has not

do not

they're

it's

won't

I am

was not

wasn't

I'm

don't

they are

hasn't

Will not

I'll

it is

Name_____ Date _____

I Am Special!

Read the message. Circle each vowel.

There is nobody just like me in the whole wide world.

Nobody smiles just like me.

Nobody draws just the way I draw.

Nobody dreams just the way I dream.

I am special!

Draw a picture to show one way you are special.

Quick Tips! Morning Message   Scholastic Professional Books

Name_____ Date _____

Story Map

I would like my story to be:

An adventure   A mystery   A fairy tale   Other _____

Main Idea

Setting

Characters

Beginning	Middle	End

Meeting the
Math Standards
With Morning Messages

Dear Students,

Today is Friday. This week we learned about counting. Look at what you are wearing. Count the pockets. Write the number on a pocket shape and sign your name.

Sincerely,

Mrs. Peabody

"Wait, I have one more pocket on my leg. That makes one, two, three, four, five pockets! I'm glad I wore these pants today. I get to write the number five. It's my favorite number!" Anna Rose spent several minutes determining where her pockets were. Then she counted them, discovered one more, and counted again. She used one-to-one correspondence and counted with accuracy. She was able to write the number five without looking at a number chart, and her formation of the number was appropriate.

Based on her excited comments, it's clear that Anna Rose was having fun responding to the math problem in that day's morning message. A morning message with math connections is a great opportunity to practice skills, assess progress, and strengthen problem-solving strategies. Following are ideas for using morning messages to teach number and operations, patterns and algebra, geometry and spatial sense, and measurement.

Number and Operations

Following the format in the sample message below, try these morning message math connections for reinforcing number and operations skills and concepts, including those involving place value and money.

Good Morning, Children!

Yesterday we finished the fourth Pixie Tricks book. There are eight books in this series. How many more books will we need to read to finish the series? Discuss this with a classmate.

Sincerely,
Mr. Mack

The language of math is often confusing for many students, even those who appear to be very comfortable with numbers and computation. Using math stories as part of your morning message will help children make a natural step in extending their literacy and comprehension skills.

○ ○ ○

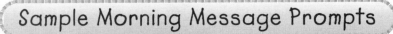

Sample Morning Message Prompts

◎ Choose a picture card. Count the number of objects and write that number in a square.

NOTE TO TEACHER: *To make picture cards, cut index cards into fourths and draw pictures such as stars, smiley faces, and hearts on them. Or use stickers.*

◎ Roll the dice. Count the number of dots and write that number next to your name.

NOTE TO TEACHER: *Place dice near the message.*

◎ Write the number that is one more [two more, five more, ten more] than the one next to your name.

NOTE TO TEACHER: *Write each child's name and a number below the message.*

◎ Write the number that is one less [two less, five less, ten less] than the one next to your name.

NOTE TO TEACHER: *Write each child's name and a number below the message.*

◎ Are there more tables or chairs in our room? Count them and write each number and your name under a sticky note in the columns labeled Tables and Chairs.

NOTE TO TEACHER: *For an independent follow-up, make copies of On My Own: Count Around, page 44.*

◎ How many people are in your family? Write that number next to your name. Draw a picture.

Count Around, page 44

◎ Write five numbers that you see in the room. List them in order from smallest to largest.

◎ Find a number in the classroom that is greater than 10. Draw a picture of the place you found it. Try to find a number that is different from everyone else's!

◎ Count backward from 10 to 0. Write the numbers on a rocket ship and tape it to our launchpad on the message.

NOTE TO TEACHER: Photocopy the rocket patterns on page 45. Cut them apart and clip to the morning message.

Rocket Ship Templates, page 45

◎ Write a number that is greater than 10 and less than 30.

◎ How many steps is it from the door to where you sit? Write the number in a footprint and sign your name.

NOTE TO TEACHER: Draw a footprint for each child.

◎ If a mother polar bear had 3 cubs and another mother had 2 cubs, how many cubs are there all together? Mark an X in the correct column.

NOTE TO TEACHER: Set up columns headed 1, 2, 3, 4, 5, 6, 7.

◎ Roll the number cubes. Use the numbers you roll to make an addition sentence. Write your addition sentence next to your name. Solve the problem!

NOTE TO TEACHER: For an independent follow-up, see On My Own: Roll, Write, Add!, page 46.

Roll, Write, Add!, page 46

◎ Draw a picture of what is happening in this math story: Five robins landed in a tree. A cat wandered near the tree and two robins flew away. How many robins stayed?

Tip

Tape a number line and hundreds board near or on the morning message board. Have appropriate math manipulatives available for students to use when building larger numbers.

○ ○ ○

Book Link

Counting **Cranes**, by Mary Beth Owens (Little, Brown, 1993), is a delightful story that combines counting with the struggle of the endangered North American whooping crane. This book provides counting practice to 15, a significant number in the history of the whooping crane. Pair this story with a morning message that invites children to count to 15 and circle sets of 15 items.

◎ I have some grapes and carrot sticks for a snack. How many of each could I have if I have 18 all together? Draw your solution on one of the plates below.

◎ Seven students are swinging on the swings. Four of them are girls. How many are boys? Draw a picture to show your answer.

◎ Write a one-digit [two-digit, three-digit] number in the space provided for you.

◎ Write a two-digit [three-digit] number that is greater than _____ and less than _____.

◎ Look at the number next to your name. Circle the digit that is in the [ones/tens/hundreds] place.

◎ Roll the dice. Using the chart below as a place value guide, write the number in a box.

NOTE TO TEACHER: *Provide dice in three different colors. Adapt the chart below accordingly.*

Blue die	Red die	Green die
hundreds	tens	ones

◎ Look at the coins on the table. Make a coin rubbing of a penny [a nickel, a dime, and so on]. Write the value of the coin on your paper. Tape the paper to the message.

◎ Draw a picture of something you think you could buy with $4.00.

Patterns and Algebra

The practice of noticing, copying, creating, and extending patterns is the work of children at all levels of mathematics. Incorporate patterns into morning messages to provide practice with this skill and to let children share their mathematical thinking with peers. Using the sample below as a model, try the variations that follow to create morning messages that build patterning skills.

Good Morning, Pattern Pals,

Today is Monday, September 24. Use the cubes to make a pattern with three colors. Add your pattern to the train on the floor.

Sincerely,

Mrs. Farnham

Sample Morning Message Prompts

◎ Draw an AB [ABC, AAB, and so on] pattern in the rectangle that has your name on it.

NOTE TO TEACHER: Include a rectangle around each child's name, along with a sample pattern.

◎ Take a strip of paper and design a pattern on it. Tape together the ends to make a headband to wear!

NOTE TO TEACHER: Clip long strips of sturdy paper, precut to headband size, to the morning message, one per child.

It's Halloween! Draw pumpkin faces to make a pattern.

NOTE TO TEACHER: *Patterns are fun ways to incorporate the holidays. Suggest other symbols for patterning as you approach holiday times.*

What would come next in this pattern? XXOOXX. Fill in only one space.

NOTE TO TEACHER: *Draw lines to indicate spaces for children to continue the pattern.*

Look around the room. Find something that makes a pattern. Draw a picture of it below.

Can you create a clapping pattern with a partner? Practice, and we will share it at meeting time.

1 + 1 = 2, 1 + 2 = 3, 1 + 3 = 4. What is the rule for this pattern? Talk it over with a classmate and write the rule together on a card. Sign your names and put the card in the box next to the message.

Geometry and Spatial Sense

Happy Wednesday, Boys and Girls,

Today is November 28. Many objects are the shape of circles. Look through the magazines and cut out something that is the shape of a circle. Glue it to the bottom of the message paper. Sign your name!

Sincerely,
Miss Chang

Place a finely crafted quilt in front of a group of children and without fail they will notice shape and symmetry as well as other beautiful details. Learning to look at the world in two and three dimensions allows children to understand mathematics not just as number but also as shape. Developing confidence with geometric vocabulary and skills can be an easy goal to meet when using morning messages with a geometric flair. Use the sample on page 40 as a model, and substitute any of the following to make geometry connections.

Sample Morning Message Prompts

◉ Draw a triangle.

NOTE TO TEACHER: *Choose one shape a day for children to practice drawing on the message.*

◉ Name something in the room shaped like a triangle [circle, square, rhombus, and so on]. Bring a friend over to see it. Place a check mark next to your name when you have followed these directions.

◉ Draw a sun using one circle and eight triangles. Be creative. Your sun does not have to look the same as anyone else's.

◉ Find something in the classroom that is the same shape as a ball. Draw a picture of it.

◉ Put your hand in the mystery box. Feel the shape. Draw what you think it is.

NOTE TO TEACHER: *A mystery box can take many forms—a box with a hole cut in it, a paper bag, even a sock!*

Book Link

In *Measuring Penny*, by Loreen Leedy (Holiday House, 1997), Lisa's homework is to measure something—anything—in as many ways as she can. When she gets home, Lisa is greeted by her dog, Penny, and decides that Penny will be the subject of her homework. Give students the same assignment, and in a morning message ask them to sign their names and tell what they measured. Use students' measurement experiences and data as a springboard for a math lesson.

Measurement

Measurement (weight, length, volume, temperature, and time) is intriguing, yet can be confusing to young children. Children will gain proficiency at all levels when allowed to experience, test, and practice the mechanics and concepts of measurement. Supplementing children's math experiences by incorporating measurement into the morning message adds precious time for practice. Use the sample below as a model for incorporating any of the following measurement activities into your morning message.

Dear Children,

I have a problem and I hope you can help me. Mr. Murray, our principal, would like to borrow our science table. I'm not sure if it will fit through the door. Please try to figure out if we can lend him our table.

Thanks,

Mrs. Adams

Sample Morning Message Prompts

- Measure your foot using the cubes. Place the cube train on the table. Write your name on a sticky note and place it on your train of cubes.

- Use your hand from the tip of your longest finger to the beginning of your wrist to measure how long the science table is. How many of your hands long is it? Trace your hand and write the number inside.

◎ Which do you think is longer: the bookshelf or the writing center table? Write your name in the appropriate column.

◎ Using the balance scale, find an object that is heavier [lighter] than the apple.

NOTE TO TEACHER: Place a balance scale on a flat surface close to the message. Have an apple and other objects available for children to weigh.

◎ Use the scale to find one object in the classroom that weighs about one pound. Draw a picture of it below.

◎ What do you think the temperature will be today? Color the thermometer next to your name.

NOTE TO TEACHER: Draw an outline of a thermometer next to each child's name. Have children color a red line and write the temperature in numbers on the thermometer.

◎ Draw a picture of yourself on the playground when the temperature is 32° F.

◎ What time do you go to bed: 7:00 P.M., 7:30 P.M., 8:00 P.M., 8:30 P.M., Other? Tape one of the pillows in the column under your bedtime.

NOTE TO TEACHER: Provide small construction paper squares for pillows. For a follow-up, see On My Own: What's the Time?, page 47.

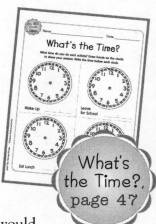

What's the Time?, page 47

◎ Look at the clock drawn on the message. How would that time look on a digital clock? Write it under a sticky note and sign your name on the front.

◎ Today we will _____. Predict how long you think it will take. Write your prediction in one of the circles.

◎ In which month do you celebrate your birthday? Color a birthday balloon and place it on the message under that month.

NOTE TO TEACHER: Photocopy the balloon patterns on page 48. Set up a birthday chart as part of the morning message, listing months across and providing space for children to add their balloon.

◎ How many more days until _____?

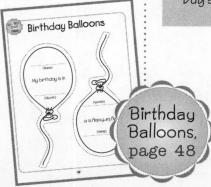

Birthday Balloons, page 48

Book Link

The Grouchy Ladybug, by Eric Carle (HarperCollins, 1996), intergrates concepts of time into a story about a mannerless ladybug. By the end of this insect's day, children see a ladybug that learns how to be considerate of others. Pair this story with a morning message that invites children to tell what they are doing at the time of each of the ladybug's encounters.

Name_____ Date _____

Count Around

Count how many of each item you find. Write the number in the box.
Find one more thing to count. Write what you count and how many there are.

Item	How Many
desks	
chairs	
windows	
children	
teachers	
cubbies	
walls	

Rocket Ship Templates

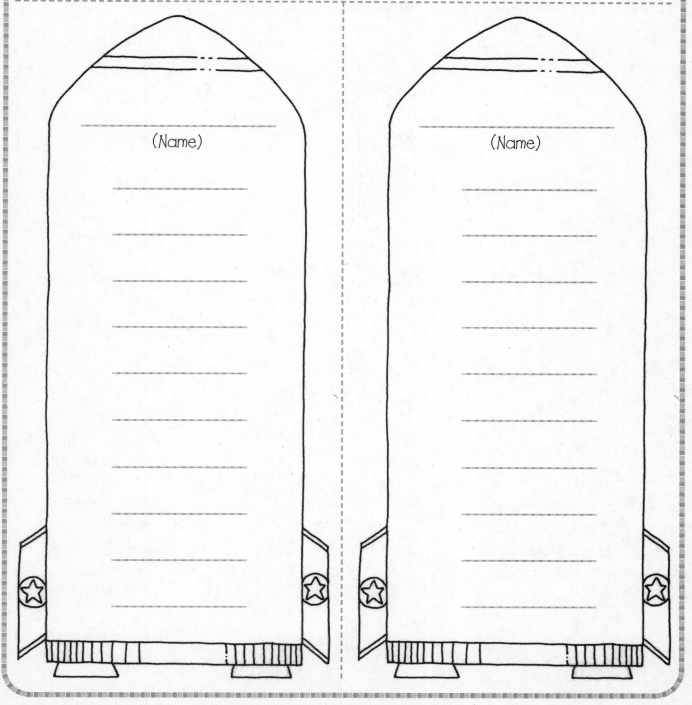

(Name)

(Name)

Name _____   Date _____

Roll, Write, Add!

Roll the number cube four times. Write each number you roll in a square.
Once you have filled all four squares, solve the addition problem.

☐ + ☐ + ☐ + ☐ = ☐

☐ + ☐ + ☐ + ☐ = ☐

☐ + ☐ + ☐ + ☐ = ☐

☐ + ☐ + ☐ + ☐ = ☐

Quick Tips! Morning Message   Scholastic Professional Books

Name_____   Date _____

What's the Time?

What time do you do each activity? Draw hands on the clocks
to show your answer. Write the time below each clock.

Wake Up   _____ : _____

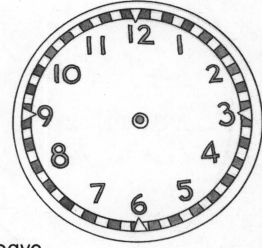

Leave
for School   _____ : _____

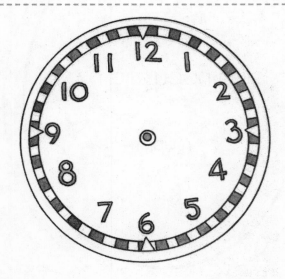

Eat Lunch   _____ : _____

Other Activity _____

_____ : _____

Birthday Balloons

_____
(Name)

My birthday is in

_____
(Month)

(Month)
_____

My birthday is in

_____
(Name)

Quick Tips! Morning Message   Scholastic Professional Books

Strengthening Science Concepts
With Morning Messages

Dear Students,

Did your seeds sprout? Check
them to find out! How many days
have passed since you planted
them? Write your name under the
number of days below.

Sincerely,
Ms. Shelton

Use morning messages
that ask children to
think scientifically
to make natural
curriculum connections.
For example, in the
boxed sample message
on page 50, children
combine the science of
seasons with math
(calendar concepts),
literacy (reading and
writing), and
art (drawing).

○ ○ ○

Each morning Carrie rushes into the classroom to see if the seeds the class planted have sprouted. They have! She checks the previous day's morning message to count how many children predicted that they would sprout today. She looks at her science log to see when the class planted the seeds, and counts the days it took them to sprout.

Students are fascinated by the world around them and long for answers to their questions. Morning messages can provide opportunities for children to make predictions, formulate responses to questions, and share scientific knowledge they've acquired. Here's how to use morning messages to support science investigations about seasons, animals, the senses, and health, plus a quick look at morning messages in five additional areas.

Seasons

Children are aware of the seasons simply by looking out the classroom window. Morning messages can focus children's observations, encouraging connections between the seasons and the world around them. Here are some seasonal morning messages that you can adapt to match your location.

Tip

Seek out pen pals in different parts of the country. Compare the differences in the seasons where they live.

○ ○ ○

Good Morning, Everyone!

Today is Thursday, December 1.
Jack Frost is busy these days!
Brrrrrrrr! It is cold. Draw something you wore to stay warm
on the way to school. Label it.
            Sincerely,
            Mrs. Sondi

Sample Morning Message Prompts

◎ Put an X by your favorite season.

   NOTE TO TEACHER: *Chart the seasons.*

◎ Will it snow today? Make a prediction: Yes or no?

◎ Were you surprised to see snow this morning? Draw a snowflake. Write Yes or No in the snowflake.

❂ It's spring. The insects are waking up! Have you seen any? Draw a picture of one. Print its name.

❂ April showers bring May flowers. Draw a raindrop. Write a word about rain inside. Draw a flower. Write a word about flowers inside.

❂ When it is summer where we live, it is winter in another place. Look at the map. Print the name of a place where the seasons are opposite ours.

❂ Look at the leaves. Describe a pattern you see. Draw it.

NOTE TO TEACHER: Tape several leaves around the border of the morning message.

❂ You dress in a different way for each season. On an activity page, color the child to show the clothes you might wear for each season. Draw a picture of what you see in each season.

NOTE TO TEACHER: Photocopy a class set of On My Own: The Seasons and Me, page 60.

The Seasons and Me, page 60

Book Link

In **The Song**, by Charlotte Zolotow (Greenwillow, 1982), a young girl listens to the song of a bird as it sings through the seasons. Pair this story with **This Year's Garden**, by Cynthia Rylant (Bradbury, 1984), to follow a family's gardening adventures through the seasons. In a morning message, invite children to draw or name a sign of winter, spring, summer, and fall. Label four areas under the message, one for each season.

Animals

Children adore animals! They are always eager to share stories about family pets, a neighbor's guinea pig, or an insect they spotted. The animal world inspires careful observations, thoughtful predictions, and passionate exploration on the part of young minds. A study of animals is also a natural springboard to an investigation of habitats. Morning messages, such as those that follow, provide tantalizing invitations into the science of animals, including their habitats.

Good Morning, Animal Lovers,

Today is Monday, January 16. We will be learning about pets this week. How do people care for pets? Draw a picture.

Sincerely,
Mr. Tenney

Sample Morning Message Prompts

- Some animals are tame and some are wild. Some are good for pets and some are not. Look at the magazines. Cut out a picture of an animal that would make a good pet. Glue it on the morning message.

- We are learning about baby animals. Write the name for a baby animal you know. Draw a picture.

  NOTE TO TEACHER: For an independent follow-up, give children copies of On My Own: Baby Animal Matchup, page 61.

  Baby Animal Matchup, page 61

- Look at the animal pictures. Draw a circle around one and write your name in it. Does your animal have fur, scales, or feathers? Put an X under the correct word.

  NOTE TO TEACHER: Cut out pictures of various animals, such as dogs, cats, ducks, lizards, fish, birds, bears, and monkeys, and tape or glue them to the morning message. Make a chart with the headings Fur, Scales, and Feathers.

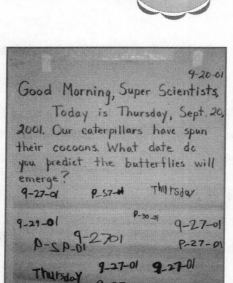

- Our caterpillars have spun their cocoons. On what date do you predict the butterflies will emerge?

- Complete the sentence: A _____ is a home for a _____ .

- Draw or write the name of an animal that lives in one of these habitats: Ocean, Meadow, Forest, Pond.

Book Link

Share *"Mine Will," Said John*, by Helen V. Griffith (Greenwillow, 1980), to learn how John finally gets the pet of his dreams. Pair the story with this morning message: Draw a picture of the pet of your dreams. What would you name your pet? Write the name next to your name.

Five Senses

bro ccoli
I hate it!
Samantha

Hello, Children!

Today is Friday. We have tasted many foods this week during our study of the sense of taste. Take a card. Write or draw a picture of a food that you do *not* like to eat. Tape it to the message.

Sincerely,

Miss Weinberg

Scientists use all of their senses to observe, question, predict, and test. An exploration of the five senses naturally provides children with a foundation for learning how to be a scientist. Here are some ready-to-use morning messages to support an investigation of the five senses.

Sample Morning Message Prompts

◎ Here are some outlines of eyes. Choose one set and draw your eyes. Use the mirror to help you see the color of your eyes.

◎ Observe the object on the tray. On a sheet of paper, draw a detailed picture of what you see.

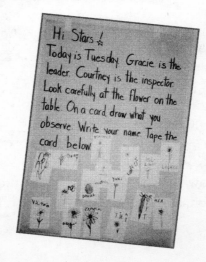

Hi Stars!
Today is Tuesday. Gracie is the leader. Courtney is the inspector. Look carefully at the flower on the table. On a card draw what you observe. Write your name. Tape the card below.

◎ Draw a picture of a favorite fruit. Write a word that describes how it tastes.

◎ Write one word that describes what a [leaf, caterpillar, snowflake, insect, and so on] looks like.

◎ Draw a picture of something that makes a loud [soft] sound.

◎ Draw a picture of something you heard on the way to school today.

◎ We will all investigate how different animals make sounds. Write the animal whose sound you want to learn more about. Be sure to write your name or initials, too!

◎ Go to your science journal. Draw three things whose sounds you like to hear. Label them.

◎ Smell a container. Under the sticky note with your name, write the number of the container and what you think is inside.

NOTE TO TEACHER: Number small containers such as empty film canisters and place fragrant objects such as small flowers, cinnamon, licorice, and peppermint in them. Cover the canisters with cheesecloth and secure with a rubber band. Place on a tray near the message.

◎ Use the finger alphabet and practice spelling your name.

NOTE TO TEACHER: Place the Sign Language Finger Alphabet on the message easel. See page 62.

As you teach each of the senses, make a list of words used to describe smells, tastes, textures, sounds, and sights. Keep these lists available for children to refer to as they interact with the morning message.

Tip

As you teach each of the senses, make a list of words used to describe smells, tastes, textures, sounds, and sights. Keep these lists available for children to refer to as they interact with the morning message.

○ ○ ○

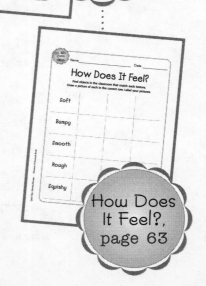

Sign Language Finger Alphabet, page 62

◎ Choose one object from the table. Place it in the basket labeled with the word that best describes what your object feels like.

NOTE TO TEACHER: Label baskets with texture words such as smooth, hard, soft, bumpy, *and* rough. *For independent exploration of textures, see On My Own: How Does It Feel?, page 63.*

◎ Find an interesting texture in the room. Make a crayon rubbing.

How Does It Feel?, page 63

Healthy Choices

> Good Morning, Healthy Children!
>
> Today is Thursday, October 31. What did you have for breakfast? Draw a picture. Tape it to the part of the food pyramid in which it belongs.
>
> Sincerely,
>
> Mr. Basset

An important aspect of a child's education is to develop healthy lifestyle habits. The science of exercise and nutrition provides information and experiences for children to begin to make healthy choices. Here's a list of interactive morning messages to support your study.

Sample Morning Message Prompts

◎ What is your favorite healthy food? Draw it or write its name on paper and tape it to the message.

◎ Choose a picture from the basket. Tape it to the correct section of the food pyramid.

NOTE TO TEACHER: Draw and label the food pyramid on the morning message.

◎ Is brushing your teeth a healthy habit? Write your name on a toothbrush. Tape it under Yes or No.

NOTE TO TEACHER: Make toothbrush templates for this morning message.

- Draw a picture to show a healthy habit you have.

- Look at the grocery store advertisements. Cut out a picture of a healthy snack you would like to eat.

- Look for the exercise station cards around the room. There are five. Follow the directions at each exercise station to get off to a healthy start today.

  NOTE TO TEACHER: Place five exercise station cards around the room with an exercise on each—for example: Do five jumping jacks.

- Complete this statement: Today at recess I plan to _____. Write your plan on a sticky note and place it on the message.

  NOTE TO TEACHER: This morning message encourages children to make connections between their recess activity and the ways they get exercise.

- There are paper plates and magazines for you on the art table. Plan a healthy meal for your family. Cut out and glue pictures to your plate.

More Science Connections

Here's a quick look at five more science areas, and some sample morning messages to support students' learning.

The Sun, Moon, Stars

Outer space intrigues children of all ages. Morning messages give children many opportunities to ponder the universe and share information about space.

Sample Morning Message Prompts

- Write the name of the planet we live on. Draw a picture to show something special about this planet.

- What do you think the moon will look like tonight? Draw a picture.

  NOTE TO TEACHER: In the following day's morning message, children can draw the moon they saw the night before and compare.

> **Tip**
>
> Help children read the nutrition labels on the foods they bring in for snacks. You might begin by showing them the difference in grams of sugar among different foods.

Changes

Changes, such as those that happen when the temperature rises and a snowman melts, capture children's curiosity. Explore changes in temperature with messages like these:

◎ Draw a picture of something you like to do when it is 90°F [45°F, 10°F] outside.

◎ Draw something that reminds you of this word: *cold.*

◎ Draw something that reminds you of this word: *hot.*

Light and Shadow

Young scientists are fascinated by shadows—their own and the ones in the world around them—and by light and the reflections they see. Use morning messages like the ones that follow to help teach these concepts.

◎ Draw a shadow for one object below.

> **NOTE TO TEACHER:** *Include simple drawings, stickers, or cutout pictures on the message.*

◎ It's cloudy today. The prism hanging in our window isn't reflecting much light. Please draw a color coming from the prism below.

> **NOTE TO TEACHER:** *Draw a picture of a prism.*

Dinosaurs

The potential for integrating the study of dinosaurs with morning messages is limitless. These sample messages invite children to respond using art.

- ☺ Scientists now think that dinosaur skin was very colorful. What do you think dinosaur skin may have looked like? Color the dinosaur outline next to your name.

- ☺ A Tyrannosaurus Rex tooth was seven inches long. Use a ruler to draw a T Rex tooth.

- ☺ Stegosaurus had lots of bony plates on its back. The one I have drawn below is missing its plates. Help complete the Stegosaurus by drawing one plate on its back.

Plants

Plants, flowers, and all things that grow are part of a child's hands-on science "laboratory." Using messages like the samples that follow enables you to use the morning message to support a study of plant science, or botany.

- ☺ Illustrate and label your favorite fruit [vegetable, tree, flower].

- ☺ Look at the leaves. Choose one and write a word that describes it. Try to use a word nobody else has already written.

    Note to Teacher: *Gather several leaves of different sizes and shapes from the ground and glue them beneath the message to make a chart. Have children record their words beneath the leaf they choose.*

- ☺ How many days do you think it will take for this seed to sprout? Write your estimate (guess) next to your name. We will see!

- ☺ Look at the picture of the tree. Write your name on one part. Label the part.

Name _____ Date _____

The Seasons and Me

Draw a picture of you outdoors in each season.
What are you wearing? What do you see?

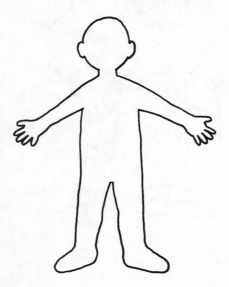

Winter

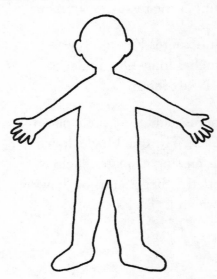

Spring

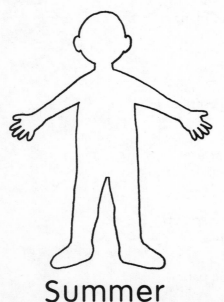

Summer

Fall

Name _____

Date _____

Baby Animal Matchup

cow 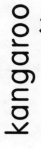  bear  kangaroo dog  frog

cub 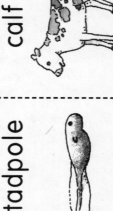 joey  calf  tadpole puppy

Name _____

Date _____

Sign Language Finger Alphabet

 A

 B

 C

 D

 E

 F

 G

 H

 I

 J

 K

 L

 M

 N

 O

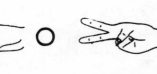 P

 Q

 R

 S

 T

 U

 V

 W

 X

 Y

Z  Z

Quick Tips! Morning Message   Scholastic Professional Books

Name_____ Date _____

How Does It Feel?

Find objects in the classroom that match each texture.
Draw a picture of each in the correct row. Label your pictures.

Soft			
Bumpy			
Smooth			
Rough			
Squishy			

Celebrating Special Days
With Morning Messages

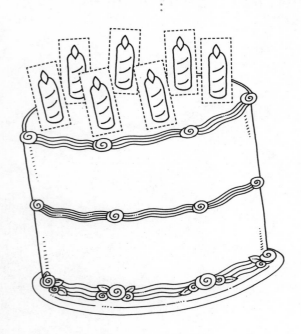

Good Morning, Class!

Today is Monday, October 8. Happy birthday, Polly! She is six years old. Write a birthday wish for Polly.

Sincerely,

Miss Ahari

It's Polly's birthday! She hurries over to the morning message, where she knows she'll find something special. Her teacher has written a birthday wish for her. The message invites Polly's classmates to do the same. Polly looks forward to the end of the day, when she knows she can bring the message full of birthday wishes home to share with her family.

How often does a teacher hear "My birthday is in a few days! I can't wait! Can I bring in a treat to share with the class?" As children weave their way through the school year, the classroom calendar is filled with landmarks in recognition of special days. These days are welcome reference points that break the daily routine and give children something to look forward to. They are magical days that offer endless possibilities for teaching about the calendar, history, diversity, customs, and traditions. Special days lend themselves to unique morning messages that invite each child's personal touch. They provide a springboard for joyful learning!

Birthdays

> Dear Children,
>
> Today is Jessica's birthday. Happy birthday, Jessica! How many months after Jessica's birthday is your birthday? Write your name under the number.
>
> > Sincerely,
> > Mr. Murray
>
> 0 1 2 3 4 5 6 7 8 9 10 11 12

Birthdays are days that students anxiously await! Even summer birthdays can be celebrated so that all children have the opportunity to have their birthday recognized on the morning message. Here are some skill-building morning messages for your birthday celebrations.

Sample Morning Message Prompts

◎ Anya is seven years old today. Write how old you will be on your next birthday.

> **NOTE TO TEACHER:** *Extend this morning message activity by inviting children to decorate their own birthday cake, complete with a message and the correct number of candles. This activity strengthens writing skills and reinforces counting skills and one-to-one correspondence.*

◎ Today is [child's name]'s birthday. Write a birthday message to [child's name].

Birthday Cake Pattern, page 76

Today is Monday, September 15. It is Giancarlo's birthday. Here's another way to express the number 15: 8 + 7. Write the date of your birthday in another way.

What is your favorite food to eat at a birthday party? Take a cupcake graph marker. Write your name on it and your favorite birthday treat. Glue it on the graph.

NOTE TO TEACHER: *Photocopy the cupcake graph marker for each child. Set up a graph near the morning message for students to record their favorite birthday foods.*

Graph Marker

A cupcake is a fun birthday treat. *Cupcake* is made up of two words: *cup* and *cake*. Write another word that is formed by putting two words together. Draw a picture!

Write the name of the month your birthday is in. Write the month that comes just before it and just after it.

Richard is six years old today! Ten more children in the class are six. The rest are seven. How many are seven? Draw a picture to show your answer.

Halloween

As soon as the calendar has changed to October, there's excitement in the air! The classroom becomes rich with art projects, special stories, and jack-o'-lanterns with wide grins. Use your morning messages to count down to Halloween, compare pumpkins, and enrich vocabulary. Here are some Halloween messages that connect with literacy, math, art, and more.

Hi, Superstars!

Today is Friday, October 21.
Guess how many seeds are in our
class pumpkin. Write your name
and your guess. This afternoon
we will open the pumpkin and
count the seeds!
                    Sincerely,
                    Mr. Oh

Sample Morning Message Prompts

◉ Print the word *Halloween* using orange and black markers. Write one word you can make with the letters in *Halloween*.

◉ We will explore sinking and floating today. Do you think a pumpkin will sink or float? Write your name under Sink or Float. Be ready to share why you think so at Morning Meeting.

◉ How many days until Halloween? Write the number next to your name.

Tip

Match the color of your morning messages to the season. Orange and black for October is fun! Attach seasonal pictures around the border for added appeal.

○ ○ ○

Book Link

Scary, Scary Halloween, by Eve Bunting (Clarion, 1986), is a short and poetic story with rich language and colorful illustrations. It's a great story to read after children share what they are going to be on Halloween. For more fun with language, pair this story with a morning message that invites children to play with words—for example: What rhymes with *bat*? Write a word below.

◎ Trace and cut out a pumpkin. Write the date of Halloween on one side. Write an [addition, subtraction] sentence that equals that date. Tape your pumpkin by the stem to the morning message.

> **NOTE TO TEACHER:** *Provide pumpkin templates (below) for children to trace.*

◎ Make a pattern using the Halloween pictures. Cut them out and glue them to your strip of paper. Tape your strip to the morning message when you are finished.

> **NOTE TO TEACHER:** *Photocopy On My Own: Halloween Patterns, page 77. Place the copies along with strips of adding machine tape beside the message.*

◎ Draw a pumpkin under your favorite type of jack-o'-lantern face.

> **NOTE TO TEACHER:** *Set up a graph for Happy, Sad, Silly, Spooky.*

Halloween Patterns, page 77

Pumpkin Template

Thanksgiving

Hello, Children!

Today is Friday, November 18.
Would you like to have sailed on
the <u>Mayflower</u> with the Pilgrims?
Sign your name under Yes or No.

Sincerely,

Miss Berkin

Before Thanksgiving invite children's families to school for dessert. Arrange to have tastings of pies to share. (Invite families to bring them. Check for food allergies before serving.) Make a family graph of favorite pies. Children can take turns sharing what they are thankful for.

○ ○ ○

Thanksgiving morning messages are an effective tool to teach history, geography, and the concepts of past and present. Messages can focus on food, sharing, and gratitude. Here are some quick-and-easy Thanksgiving morning messages to use.

Sample Morning Message Prompts

◎ Draw a picture of something you are thankful for.

Book Link

I n *Thanksgiving at the Tappleton's*, by Eileen Spinelli (Harper, 1982), the Tappleton family experiences some unexpected events. Children will learn about the importance of family in this lively story. Pair this story with a morning message that invites children to tell why they would or would not like to have Thanksgiving with the Tappleton family.

◎ What is your favorite Thanksgiving pie? Write your name on the graph to show your answer.

NOTE TO TEACHER: *Set up a simple graph on the morning message for pie types, including Pumpkin, Apple, Cherry, Mincemeat, Pecan, and I Don't Like Pie!*

◎ Look at the three pies. Think of a way to divide them so that each child in our class gets a slice and there are no slices left over. Tell how many pieces you will cut each pie into.

NOTE TO TEACHER: *Draw three pies beneath the morning message.*

◎ Thanksgiving is always on the same day of the week. Use a calendar to find out what date it is on this year. Print your answer on the back of the sticky note with your name.

◎ Draw a picture of something you have in your home that a Pilgrim child would not have had. Label it.

Pilgrims didn't have a washing machine.

◎ Look at the map by the easel. Plymouth, Massachusetts, is circled. That is where the *Mayflower* landed. Write the name of a place that is near Plymouth.

◎ Copy the word *Thanksgiving* below. Underline words you see in this word.

◎ Think of Thanksgiving foods people eat. Draw a picture of one in the food pyramid.

NOTE TO TEACHER: *Draw a large food pyramid beneath the message.*

Winter Holidays

Dear Stars!

Today is Thursday, December 15. We can all lend a helping hand when somebody needs it. Trace your hand on the morning message paper. Write one way you can help someone today.

Sincerely,

Mrs. Jacobs

December is a month rich in customs and traditions. It is a time to use morning messages to stress the importance of giving, reaching out to others, and celebrating each student's heritage. Here are some ready-to-use morning messages to reinforce the holiday spirit.

Sample Morning Message Prompts

- People have many customs and traditions. Does your family celebrate a holiday in December? Write the name or a symbol for the holiday.

- We are making wrapping paper. Please help by stamping some patterns on a sheet of paper.

    NOTE TO TEACHER: *Set out several sheets of paper with sponge stamps and paints. Have children create a colorful pattern on the paper with the sponge stamps.*

- Draw a picture of a special food your family makes in December. Write words that describe how it looks, smells, and tastes.

Holiday
Bookmark,
page 78

◎ Think of someone who works at our school and helps you. Print this person's name on the message. Make a thank-you bookmark for this person.

NOTE TO TEACHER: *Photocopy the bookmark pattern on page 78 for children to use. Have them cut along the dotted lines, fold on the solid center line, and glue the bookmark together.*

◎ Draw a picture of yourself helping at home. Draw a picture of someone helping you.

◎ Everyone is good at doing something at school. If someone needs help, he or she might come to you and ask for it. Finish this sentence and sign your name: I can help you _____.

NOTE TO TEACHER: *Write this sentence starter on the message once for each child.*

◎ What is a gift you can give someone that doesn't cost any money? Write your idea inside a box.

Valentine's Day

Good Morning!

Today is Tuesday, February 13. Tomorrow is Valentine's Day! I will bake cupcakes for our party. What color frosting do you like best? Draw a heart by your choice.

     Sincerely,

     Mrs. Baker-Leidy

Red   Pink   White

Valentine's Day morning messages can teach concepts of friendship and appreciation. Here are morning messages to explore these themes. The messages work well as springboards to class discussions during morning meetings.

Sample Morning Message Prompts

◉ Look at the calendar. How many days until Valentine's Day? Write a number sentence that has the date as an answer.

◉ Write the word *love* in a fancy way.

◉ Add on to the heart pattern. Write your initials inside your hearts.

NOTE TO TEACHER: *Start a heart pattern, using color or design to create the pattern.*

◉ Have you read a great book? Take a valentine. Fill in the blanks to tell about your book. Give it to a classmate!

NOTE TO TEACHER: *Photocopy On My Own: I Love Books!, page 79, for children to complete.*

I Love Books!, page 79

◉ Write one way you show someone in your family your love. Write one way someone shows love to you.

◉ Add a line to the poem by listing something that is red.

NOTE TO TEACHER: *Start a class list poem with the words "Red is..." Draw a fill-in line for each child to complete. Share another poem about the color red: "What Is Red?" from* Hailstones and Halibut Bones: Adventures in Color *by Mary O'Neill (Doubleday, 1990).*

◉ Draw a valentine heart. Write a friendly message in it.

◉ What word can you make with the letters in *valentine*? Write it next to your name.

Book Link

"**W**riter cats get ready, writer cats start a card, writer cats need a message..." There's lots to like about **Valentine Cats**, by Jean Marzollo (Scholastic, 1996), including reading the cats' cards, which fill several pages. Pair this rhyming story with a morning message that lets children suggest valentine messages for the morning cats. Use the morning message to initiate a valentine-making activity.

The 100th Day of School

As the 100th day of school approaches, children are busily counting and looking forward to the special events planned for the day. Incorporate the 100th day theme into morning messages to teach a variety of numerical concepts. Here are some suggestions.

Tip

Save all the morning messages that are about the 100th day of school. Combine them to make a Big Book. Let children illustrate the pages and dedicate the book to next year's class.

○ ○ ○

Good Morning!

Today is Friday, February 17.
It is our 100th day together!
Write the number 100 in a way
you've never written it before.
Sincerely,
Miss Kim

Sample Morning Message Prompts

✺ Estimate the number of candies [marbles, buttons, and so on] in the jar. Do you think there are more than 100, less than 100, or exactly 100? Write your name below your answer.

More Than 100   Less Than 100   Exactly 100

✺ Fill in a missing number. Count by fives.
5, ___, ___, ___, ___, ___, ___, ___,
___, ___, ___, ___, ___, ___, ___,
___, ___, ___, ___, 100!

✺ Choose a partner and together take 100 steps around the room. Write your names together.

✺ Take a piece of string. The string is 100 centimeters long! Use it to measure objects in the classroom. What is longer? What is shorter? What is the same length? Fill in the sheet to tell what you find.

NOTE TO TEACHER: *Photocopy On My Own: Longer, Shorter, the Same, page 80.*

On My Own

Name _____ Date _____

Longer, Shorter, the Same

Item	Longer Than 100 cm	Shorter Than 100 cm	The Same as 100 cm

Longer, Shorter, the Same, page 80

✺ Use the calendar to find out what the date will be in 100 days. Write the date next to your name.

✺ What object do you think would weigh 100 pounds? Draw a picture of your guess. Label it.

✺ In what way do you think the world will be different in 100 years? Draw a picture of your idea.

✺ If you could have 100 of something, what would it be? Draw a picture or write about it.

Book Link

In *100th Day Worries,* by Margery Cuyler (Simon & Schuster, 2000), Jessica worries about what she will bring to school on the 100th day. Share this playful book with students before your 100th day celebration to help them think creatively about the number 100. In a morning message, ask: Can we think of 100 favorite things about school so far? Write the numbers 1–100 below the message, and have children write a favorite thing next to each.

Name_____   Date_____

Birthday Cake Pattern

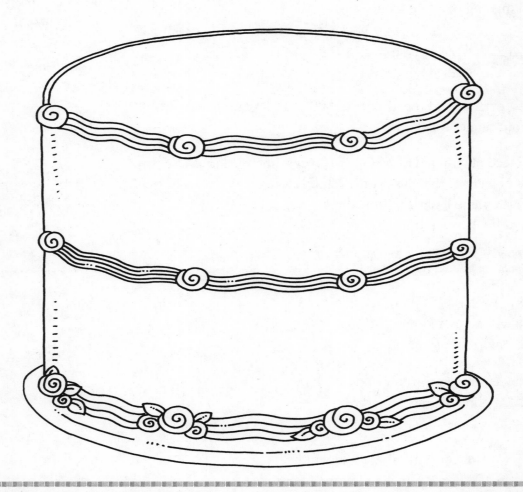

Quick Tips! Morning Message   Scholastic Professional Books

Name_____ Date _____

Halloween Patterns

Holiday Bookmark

(fold)

Happy Holidays

To: _____

From: _____

Quick Tips! Morning Message   Scholastic Professional Books

On My Own

I Love Books!

Roses are red,
Violets are blue.
I read a great book,
And so can you!

Title _____

Author _____

I LOVE this book because _____

_____

_____

_____

(Name)

Name_____ Date _____

Longer, Shorter, the Same

Item	Longer Than 100 cm	Shorter Than 100 cm	The Same as 100 cm